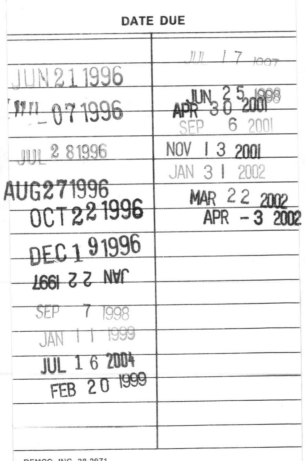

**DATE DUE**

| | |
|---|---|
| | JUL 17 1997 |
| JUN 21 1996 | |
| JUL 07 1996 | JUN 25 1998 |
| | APR 30 2001 |
| | SEP 6 2001 |
| JUL 28 1996 | NOV 13 2001 |
| | JAN 31 2002 |
| AUG 27 1996 | MAR 22 2002 |
| OCT 22 1996 | APR -3 2002 |
| DEC 19 1996 | |
| JAN 22 1997 | |
| SEP 7 1998 | |
| JAN 11 1999 | |
| JUL 16 2004 | |
| FEB 20 1999 | |
| | |
| | |

DEMCO, INC. 38-2971

## A Discovery Biography

# Davy Crockett

— ◆ —

## *Hero of the Wild Frontier*

by Elizabeth R. Moseley
*illustrated by Thomas Beecham*

**CHELSEA JUNIORS**
*A division of Chelsea House Publishers*
*New York ◆ Philadelphia*

To Marcia, Marc, Mary, Melissa, and Marshall

The Discovery Biographies have been prepared under the educational supervision of Mary C. Austin, Ed.D., Reading Specialist and Professor of Education, Case Western Reserve University.

Cover illustration: Maia Stone

First Chelsea House edition 1991

3   5   7   9   8   6   4

ISBN   0-7910-1409-6

# Contents

## Davy Crockett:
## Hero of the Wild Frontier

# Chapter *1*

## Davy

As soon as his chores were done, Davy Crockett stole off to the woods. Stepping light-footed as a deer, he followed a trail to the edge of the forest.

The nine-year-old boy hid behind a bush and sat very still. He was watching a mother bird. She was busy gathering her young ones under her wings before dark.

Davy lived in eastern Tennessee. His father had a tavern on the trail between Knoxville and Abingdon, Virginia. In 1795 the land there was still almost wilderness. There were only a few close neighbors, and no schools.

John Crockett and his wife Rebecca were very poor. They tried hard to make a living for their six boys and three girls. But paying guests at the tavern were few and far between.

Suddenly a loud clear call rang out through the woods. "Da-a-vy! Da-a-vy! Come to supper!" called Mother.

The mother quail fluttered in alarm. Davy sat still. He whispered softly. "Yes, ma'am. I'm a-coming."

The young quail ran swiftly to their mother and nestled beside her.

"Davy Crockett! You come here this instant!"

Again Davy answered her in a soft whisper. "Yes, ma'am. I'm a-coming."

Rebecca Crockett stood for a moment at the door. Then she returned to the table.

"That's the second time I've called that boy," she told her husband. "Davy would live in the woods if he could."

Just then Davy stepped through the door.

"Why didn't you answer your ma, Davy?"

"I answered, Pa."

"Did anyone hear Davy's answer?"

The young Crocketts solemnly shook their heads and looked at their plates.

"About how loud was your answer?"

Davy glanced quickly at his older brothers. They continued to pay close attention to their plates. With a sheepish look, the boy faced his father.

"Not very loud, Pa," he said. "I was watching some quail and I didn't want to scare them."

"Humph! These woods still have a few Indians in them. Eighteen years ago they killed my ma and pa right in their own cabin. When we call you, it might mean life or death. Is that clear?"

Davy nodded.

"And another thing, Davy, when you answered your ma, you knew that she couldn't hear you. Yet you told me you answered. That wasn't honest. Don't ever do that again."

"I won't, Pa."

"Now eat your supper. Some drovers will be here soon. They're driving their cattle to Virginia. You boys must be ready to bed down the herd."

Davy sat down beside his sister Jane. "Janie, do you know what I did while I watched the quail?"

"No. What?"

"Practiced grinning," Davy said with a twinkle in his eye.

"What for, Davy?"

"I'm going to out-grin a possum someday. He'll fall right down out of the tree, plumb dead. All I'll have to do is pick him up and bring him home."

Janie giggled. Davy always had a funny story to tell.

# Chapter *2*

# Davy Goes A-Traveling

"Huh-ee! Huh-ee! Get back there, you crazy old cow!" Davy was helping a man with his cattle.

Jacob Siler had stopped at Crockett's Tavern. He was a drover who bought cattle in the backwoods and drove them to Virginia to sell. He was finding it hard to manage the herd alone, and he was still 400 miles from home.

The Dutchman watched Davy as he worked. He saw the boy was quick and cheerful.

"John," he said to Mr. Crockett, "would you consider hiring out Davy to me for the rest of this drive?"

"The boy is only twelve years old, Jacob."

"But he is a pretty good worker. I'll send him back as soon as I deliver this herd."

Money was scarce in the Crockett household, and boys were not. So Mr. Crockett agreed to hire out Davy.

Before Davy left home, his mother made him a new coonskin cap. And his father gave him a rifle.

"There may be times on the trail when you'll need this, Davy," his father said. "You probably won't meet any unfriendly Indians, but you might want a rabbit or a squirrel for supper."

Davy was thrilled. "I reckon it'll come in right handy." He patted his gun proudly.

"Remember, Davy, you're only bound out to Jacob Siler for the cattle drive. Come back home as soon as you can find someone coming this way."

Poor men often hired out a child to work for another family until grown. Davy was glad he was coming home when the drive was over.

At the end of the journey, Siler paid Davy six dollars. "Now you're to help me on the farm, Davy," he said.

"But Pa told me I was to come home."

"Maybe he changed his mind, boy."

Davy did not know what to believe. But he had to obey the man.

The Dutchman kept Davy very busy. He was not unkind, but the boy was unhappy. He wanted to go home.

One Sunday, three wagons passed along the road near the Silers' house. Davy saw a neighbor from Tennessee. His name was Dunn, and he lived near Crockett's Tavern.

Davy ran into the road and waved his arms wildly. Mr. Dunn stopped his team. The boy scrambled up onto the wagon.

"Davy Crockett! Where did you come from?"

Quickly Davy explained. "Can you help me, sir? I want to go home."

Mr. Dunn scratched his head. "Davy, are you sure Siler promised to send you home at the end of the drive?"

"Yes, sir. I heard him." Tears filled Davy's eyes.

"Well, boy," said Mr. Dunn with a wink, "we're going to spend the night at the next tavern. It's about seven miles down the road. We'll be on our way again at daybreak. I could just happen to find you in one of the wagons after we're well on the way. I don't know a thing I could do about that, do you?"

"No, sir." A smile broke through the boy's tears.

Davy jumped down from the wagon and ran to the Silers' house to complete his chores. After supper he got ready for bed.

Mr. Siler was in the living room. He saw Davy start upstairs.

"Why are you going to bed so early, Davy?" Mr. Siler said. "We can't work tomorrow. It's snowing hard."

Davy yawned. "I'm sleepy, sir. I think I'll turn in."

The boy lay quiet as a mouse long after the others went to bed. Then he took his clothes which he had made into a bundle. Silently he crept down the stairs. Every step made a creaking noise. His heart beat fast. Finally, he reached the yard safely.

The snow was almost up to his knees, but the homesick boy trudged down the road. He was almost frozen when he reached the tavern where Mr. Dunn was staying. The next morning the wagon had another passenger.

Davy was on his way home at last.

# Chapter *3*

# A Short School Term

Davy looked longingly at the bright autumn woods. They seemed to be calling him. He wished he were going hunting. Instead, he was going to school.

More people had settled near Crockett's Tavern. A man named Benjamin Kitchen had started a school. John Crockett had enrolled his children.

Davy was the biggest boy who could not read or write. His brothers had learned while he was in Virginia.

One morning as he read aloud from the first reader, he heard a snicker behind him. He looked around and saw a tall teenager, named Johnny Crawford, making fun of him.

"Don't mind Johnny," Davy's neighbor whispered. "Everybody knows he is a bully. He picks on all the boys smaller than he is."

Davy frowned. "I'll get even with Johnny Crawford if it's the last thing I do," he decided.

Before classes were over, Davy left the schoolroom. He hurried along the path that led to Johnny's home. About a half mile from the Crawford house, he hid in the bushes.

When Johnny came walking by, Davy jumped out and stood before him.

Johnny was really a coward. He started to run. Davy caught him and the battle was on. Both boys were bruised and bleeding when it ended. Davy had won.

"Don't you ever bully smaller boys again. If you have to fight, pick on somebody your size. Hear me?"

"I promise I won't pick on anyone," blubbered Johnny.

Davy dusted his clothes, picked up his books and started home.

The next morning, he stared at his face in the mirror. Davy knew that Johnny's face looked worse than his. The teacher would surely punish them both for fighting. Mr. Kitchen kept a hickory stick by his desk. He whipped the boys who caused trouble.

On the way to school, Davy stopped.

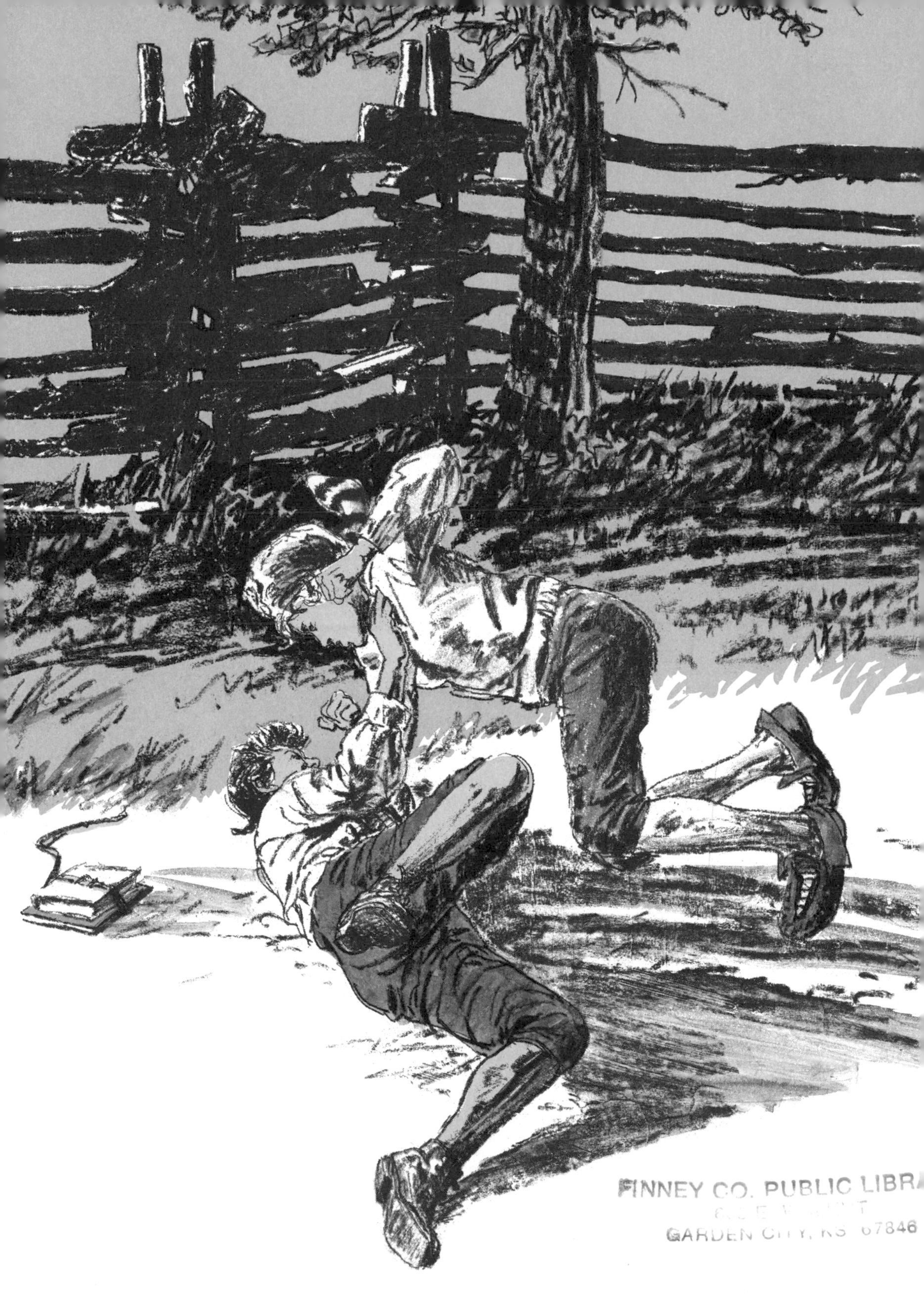

"You go on," he told his brothers. "I think I'd better stay away from school for a few days. When Mr. Kitchen sees Johnny's black eye, he'll be angry. I'll meet you here after school. Then Pa won't know I've been in the woods all day."

For four days, Davy roamed in his beloved woods. He could not use his gun. The shots would be heard at home. But he checked the traps that he and his brothers had set.

The teacher thought Davy was sick. His father thought he was in school. On the fourth day, the two men met.

"When will Davy be back in school?" asked the teacher.

"Hasn't he been in school?" Mr. Crockett said.

Mr. Kitchen shook his head. "Not for four days."

"H'm! I didn't know that. I'll look into it."

That evening when Davy finished his chores, his father was waiting for him.

"Your teacher tells me you haven't been in school. Where have you been?"

"Pa, I had a fight on the way home from school. I thought I had better let Mr. Kitchen cool off before I went back. He's pretty handy with a hickory stick."

"Fighting, huh? Well, I'm right handy with a hickory stick myself."

Mr. Crockett was angry. Davy saw that he was holding a stick in his hand. The boy turned and took to his heels with his father behind him. But Davy soon outran him. He hid in the woods.

Finally, his father gave up the chase.

"If I go home, Pa will whip me," thought Davy. "If I go to school, I'll get another whipping from Mr. Kitchen. What shall I do?"

Then he remembered that a neighbor was leaving for Virginia the next day. He was taking some cattle there. Maybe he would need a helper. With that in mind, Davy lay down on a bed of pine needles and went to sleep.

The neighbor was glad to have a helper. Soon Davy was on the road. He felt much safer as the distance widened between him and his father and his teacher.

At the end of the drive, Davy was paid four dollars. He tucked the money into his pocket. Then he made a decision.

He would stay in Virginia and work until his father's temper had cooled.

For several years, Davy supported himself by working at odd jobs. Just before his sixteenth birthday, he could stand it no longer. He was so homesick that he returned to Tennessee.

"Did you walk all the way home, Davy?" asked his father.

"Of course not," said Davy with a smile. "I just latched on to the tail of a kite and sailed in."

# Chapter *4*

# Farmer and Hunter

Davy was happy to be home. And his father seemed glad to have him back with the family once more.

One day Mr. Crockett talked to Davy. "Son, do you remember what I said when I hired you out to Jacob Siler for that wagon drive? I said I'd never hire you out again. But I just don't seem to be able to stay out of debt.

Now that your two older brothers are married, they can't help me any more. The truth of the matter is, I owe Abe Wilson 35 dollars. He wants you to work for him six months to pay it. Will you do it?"

"Sure I will, Pa. I'll be glad to help you."

Davy went to work at once.

When the six months ended, he asked a neighbor for a job on his farm.

"Davy, everybody around here knows you're honest and a good worker. I certainly could use you. But did you know your Pa owes me 40 dollars?"

"No, sir. I didn't."

"I'll tell you what I'll do. If you will work six months to pay off his debt, I'll give you a regular job."

Davy agreed to work for the man. At the end of six months, he told his father the debt was paid. Crockett looked at his son with tears in his eyes.

"Davy, this makes me mighty proud. I reckon I just don't have the knack of saving money."

One day a beautiful girl came to visit the neighbor's family. Seventeen-year-old Davy fell in love with her. Soon he asked her to marry him.

"No, Davy," she replied. "I like you, but I'm going to marry someone else. He is a schoolteacher. I gave him my promise and I won't break it."

Davy was brokenhearted. He thought he had been refused because he could not read and write. The time had come to do something about it.

The first thing Davy did was to ask his boss for help.

"One of my sons is a teacher. He will help you. Work for him two days each week and he'll give you lessons."

For several months, Davy worked hard at his lessons. He made rapid progress because he wanted to learn.

Soon he met another girl who made him forget his first love. Her name was Mary Finley. Polly, as she was called, was a pretty, blue-eyed Irish girl. Davy told his family that she was sweeter than sugar.

Davy and Polly were married in August, 1806. Their wedding presents were a spinning wheel and two cows and calves. The happy young couple rented a little farm.

Davy worked hard at farming. But hunting was his great love. He was a skilled woodsman and his family always had plenty of game to eat.

Nothing was more exciting to Davy than a bear hunt. He would go through the forests watching for a hollow tree.

Davy would walk slowly around the tree looking for bear signs. If the bark had short scratches, a bear was likely to be sleeping inside. When the scratches were long, the bear had slipped down the tree trunk and moved on.

If the bear was still there, Davy's hounds raced around the tree, barking furiously. The angry bear would climb down snarling and growling. Then Davy would call his dogs away, and take careful aim at the great beast.

Grizzly bears are very powerful and dangerous animals. Sometimes they claw hunting dogs to death. If Davy were not careful, he could be killed too. But Davy was a fine shot. He seldom missed. He called his trusty rifle Old Betsy.

Polly was always happy when Davy returned home safely. Two sons were born while the Crocketts lived in eastern Tennessee. Their names were John and William.

Before long Davy began to get restless. He complained of having to pay high rent for his farm. Deer and small game were still plentiful, but bears were getting scarce. Worst of all, too many people had moved into the area. Davy felt crowded. In the summer of 1811, he made up his mind to leave.

"Polly, pack up the kids," he said. "We're going to go west."

Before the end of September, the Crocketts were on their way to middle Tennessee. After two years, they moved again. Their new home was a few miles north of the Alabama line. To the south was the unsettled Mississippi Territory. It was still largely Indian country.

Soon a corn patch was planted. Wood was stacked beside the cabin wall. Meat was plentiful. Davy had a pile of skins ready to trade at the settlement for supplies like salt, sugar, flour, and tea. Polly and the boys were happy in their snug little home.

# Chapter *5*

# War with the Red Sticks

"I'm a-going to join the militia and get after those murdering Red Sticks," Davy told his wife. "They sure murdered a bunch of people down at Fort Mims."

Tecumseh, a powerful chief, had aroused the Creek Indians. He was trying to stop the white people from moving into the Mississippi Territory.

Indian warriors who followed the mighty Tecumseh painted their war clubs red. For this reason they were called the "Red Sticks."

The Red Sticks had attacked Fort Mims, on the lower Alabama River. They killed hundreds of men, women, and children. Now they were moving north.

"If we don't stop them, they'll soon find their way up here," said Davy.

Davy's wife hated to have him go. But she knew he had to. Soon she was packing his saddle bags and filling his powder horn. He made a final check of the meat supply.

Many Tennessee men soon joined the militia. They served under the famous Indian fighter, Andrew Jackson.

Because he was a fine woodsman, Davy was assigned to a scouting party. These men were sent to find out where the Indians were and what they were doing. The silent, swift-footed Creeks were not easy to follow in the woods. But the scouts had learned to move silently and swiftly too.

One night Davy and his partner were returning late to camp. Suddenly they saw some Red Sticks hiding their canoes around the bend of the river. From behind a tree, Davy watched them. The Indians started to creep through the woods to attack the sleeping soldiers.

Davy sent his partner to warn the men in camp. Then he slipped past the Indians. He moved their canoes and hid them without making a sound.

Just as the Indians were about to attack the camp, Davy gave a loud and fearful yell. All the soldiers joined in. The woods rang with the uproar. The Red Sticks were frightened out of their wits. They turned and ran to the river. Their canoes had disappeared! Davy gave another terrifying yell. With wild leaps, the Indians jumped into the river and escaped.

Davy served the army well. But he was happy when he could return home.

Early in 1815, a little girl was born to the Crocketts. She was called Polly.

Six months later Mrs. Crockett died after a short illness. At first Davy and his children tried to manage without help. Then Davy asked his youngest brother and his wife to come and stay.

This did not work out. So Davy began to look around for a new wife.

Soon he married Elizabeth Patton, a widow with two young children. She was a strong and sensible woman. Her husband had been killed in the war with the Red Sticks.

On the wedding day, the guests were all gathered in Elizabeth's living room waiting for the bride to appear. Davy and the minister stood, ready for the ceremony to start. Suddenly, the sound of pigs was heard. Through the doorway waddled a big fat pig, grunting every step of the way. Everyone burst into laughter. Davy quickly guided the fat uninvited visitor back through the door. He said, "Old hook, from now on I'll do the grunting around here!"

People in large numbers were coming to middle Tennessee. The woods Davy loved were being settled.

In 1817 Davy took Elizabeth and their children about 80 miles away, to Lawrence County. He opened two mills at the head of Shoal Creek. One was a powder mill, and here he made gunpowder. The other was a grist mill where grain was ground into meal or flour. Things were going well for Davy and his family.

# Chapter *6*

# Running for the Legislature

There were thick patches of tall, woody reeds growing in the Tennessee frontierland. These reeds were known as canebrakes. Often the canes were six or seven feet tall.

One morning Davy and his oldest son, with their dogs, tracked a big bear into a canebrake. Vines and briers grew around the cane stalks. Travel often became painful.

Finally, Davy got close enough to get a shot at the big beast. But Davy was hot and tired. He found it hard to hold Old Betsy steady.

Crack! The bullet crashed into the bear's shoulder. The animal turned and started moving toward him. Davy reached for his hunting knife. It was gone! He must have lost it in the thick cane. Quickly he began to reload.

Just before the bear reached him, Davy raised Old Betsy again. This time his aim was true. The bear fell just a few feet away.

Davy and his son found the hunting knife, skinned the bear, and took the meat home.

The name and fame of Davy Crockett spread over the whole Tennessee frontier.

The skilled woodsman was known to be honest and dependable. The people of Lawrence County not only trusted him, but liked him as well.

Each county had its own company of militia. These soldiers were called upon in cases of emergency. Davy became a colonel in the militia in 1818.

Later he was elected the justice of peace. After that, he became town commissioner of Lawrenceburg. This was something like being town manager. As the little town grew, there were many records to be kept. Davy now had use for his training in reading, writing, and arithmetic.

In 1821 he became a candidate for the Tennessee legislature. People flocked to hear his speeches. They loved the funny stories he mixed in with his remarks about politics. Davy told about his trained bear, Death Hug, and his pet alligator, Old Mississippi. These were imaginary animals to which he gave human abilities.

"Gentlemen," Davy said, "you ought to see Death Hug sit at the table. He eats just like a man. When he can find his glasses, he likes to read. But he's careless with those glasses. They're always getting lost.

"Old Mississippi comes in handy when I don't have a horse," he went on. "After a hard day of hunting, I just get on that old alligator and ride home fast."

"I hear you're a pretty good shot, Davy," someone in the audience shouted.

"You must be right," Davy said. "Just the other day I was walking through the woods. I spied an old coon a-sittin' on a limb. I lifted Old Betsy and drew a bead on that creature. What do you think happened? That old coon raised his paw and said, 'Are you Davy Crockett?' I nodded. 'Well, don't shoot,' he said. 'I'll come down.' Now gentlemen, I'm a modest man. When he gave up so quickly, I was embarrassed."

After Davy was elected to the legislature, he began to be uneasy.

"I don't know a thing about lawmaking," he said to his wife. "What will I do when I get to the legislature?"

"Don't worry," replied Elizabeth. "Just remember to follow your own advice, 'Be sure you're right, then go ahead.'"

# Chapter 7

# A Gentleman
## from the Cane

Colonel Davy Crockett was present in September, 1821, when the Tennessee legislature met. He had two major interests. One was to see that the poor people of west Tennessee had a chance to buy the land they had cleared. The other was to get the boundaries set on this land.

Davy was dressed in deerskin jacket and pants and wore his coonskin cap. He looked different from the other legislators.

Early in the session, he made his first speech. When he finished, a member who disagreed with him arose. This man was dressed in the height of fashion. He wore white ruffles on his shirt front and at his cuffs.

"You have heard the opinion of the gentlemen from the cane," he said with a smile and a nod toward Colonel Crockett. A wave of laughter swept through the room.

Davy sat quietly until the man finished his speech. But he decided to give the man a lesson in manners. That afternoon he found a piece of white ruffling. It was much like that on the rude man's shirt. The next day most of the members were in their seats when Davy rose to speak again.

Pinned to the front of his deerskin jacket was the white ruffle. Before he could open his mouth, the members saw the ruffle. They burst into laughter, rose to their feet, and clapped and shouted. Without saying a word, Colonel Crockett had won their respect and admiration.

When Davy returned home from this session of the legislature, he found his family worried and upset. Both mills had been swept away by a flash flood.

"Don't worry," he said, sweeping his little daughter up in his arms. "I've decided to sell this place. We'll move to the Obion River country. It's about 150 miles from here—farther west, of course. We ought to be able to have our new cabin ready by the time the next session of the legislature is over."

"Pa, are there any Indians in the Obion River country?" asked Robert.

Davy nodded. "Yes, son. There are some Chickasaws living around there, but they're friendly."

Mrs. Crockett sighed with relief. "I'm glad to hear they're friendly. I can look out for panthers, deer, and black bears. But I am mortally scared of unfriendly Indians."

"How many bears did you kill last year, Pa?" asked Robert.

"Well, son, if my count was right, I killed 105. That was 58 in the fall and winter, and 47 in the spring. Along with the buffalo and deer meat, that gave us plenty of meat, didn't it?"

"And there was some left over," said his wife.

As the children grew older, Davy needed more money. When he was home from the legislature, he decided to make barrel staves. He had to build some barges and float them on the river down to New Orleans. There was a good market there for the staves.

He hired men to help him cut down trees and saw them into barrel staves. Then he loaded them on the barges.

Piloting on the Mississippi River was a difficult job. Davy did not know it, but he had hired a pilot who was not familiar with the dangers of the river. A few miles from Memphis, all three barges went out of control and began to sink. All the men swam to safety but Davy. He was caught in a hole in the deck of the barge.

He was about to drown when two of his men saw what had happened. They returned and pulled him loose. Although he had lost a lot of money, he was happy to be alive.

His family was glad when he arrived home. Robert said, "Pa, we heard you came out of that old river just as dry as a bone. Is that true?"

With his usual courage when faced with trouble, Davy gave a big smile. "Why, of course it's true, boy," he said. "Don't you know I can run faster, dive deeper, stay under longer, and come up drier than any man in the whole of creation?"

# Chapter 8

# Colonel Crockett Goes to Congress

Davy made many friends in the state legislature. He did not hesitate to fight for what he thought was right. The people of west Tennessee liked him. After a time, they began to ask him to run for the United States Congress.

"Shucks," Davy said, "I'm not the man for that. I know nothing about national matters."

His friends continued to ask him. At last he agreed to run. But not enough time was left for his political campaign. In August, 1825, he was defeated. He began at once to work for the next election.

His opponent for Congressman from Tennessee was a skillful politician. He decided to ignore Davy. The name of Davy Crockett was never mentioned in any of his speeches.

One day the two men spoke at the same meeting. It was warm and the meeting was held out of doors.

Davy's opponent thundered and roared with big words and big promises. "You are my people," he said. "And I know when you go to the polls, you will vote for me."

In a nearby field was a flock of guinea hens.

"Pot-rack! Pot-rack! Pot-rack!" the birds called.

The loud sound of the guineas filled the air. They had wandered close to the stand and were frightened. Their clatter made it impossible for the speaker to be heard. He sat down.

When all was quiet again, Davy came forward to speak.

"I'm glad my friend here understands guinea talk," he said with a bow to his opponent. "He ignored my presence so long that everybody got tired listening to him. But it took my fine feathered friends to tell him. Those guineas made it mighty plain. They were saying, 'Crockett! Crockett! Crockett!'"

The audience laughed and shouted for more. When election day arrived, Davy Crockett was elected.

In December, 1827, Davy went to Washington. Although he dressed like everyone else in Congress, he talked like the frontiersman that he was. His clear thinking, his keen mind, and his ready wit were soon recognized. He knew that he did not know about "Congress matters." But he listened carefully, and he learned from what he heard. He was elected again in 1829.

That same year Tennessee's Andrew Jackson was elected President of the United States. At the end of the war with the Red Sticks, General Jackson had held a conference with the Creek Indian chiefs.

"You must sign a treaty," the tall General had told them. "You must give half of all your lands to the United States government. We promise that your people may keep the other half as long as they live."

The Indian chiefs were not happy, but they had signed the treaty. Now, fifteen years later, President Jackson wanted the Indians to give up all their land and move across the Mississippi.

When Davy heard about this he was very angry. "Whoever heard of that way of doing? That land belongs to the Indians. I'll fight to help them keep it."

"I don't think you should, Davy," a friend said. "Jackson won't like it."

"I don't care. It's not right. I'll fight it with every breath in my body."

"You may not be re-elected if you do," his friend warned.

"That'll be all right with me. I can always go back to hunting bears."

Davy worked hard to keep the Indians from being moved. But Congress passed the bill. The Indians were forced to set out for their new homes.

Davy had liked Andrew Jackson when Jackson was his army commander. But Davy could no longer be his friend. He could not forgive Jackson for forcing the Indians from their land. Davy spoke his mind freely. By doing so, he lost many votes when he ran for Congress again. He was not re-elected.

In spite of his disappointment, Davy continued to live by his motto, "Be sure you're right, then go ahead!"

# Chapter *9*

# "Remember the Alamo!"

Davy did return to Congress to finish his term. But when it came to an end in 1835, he was tired of politics.

"I've been knocked down and dragged out," Davy said. "Now I'm done with politics for the present. I'm going to Texas!"

Davy Crockett was a frontiersman. The frontier was moving west, and he wanted to move with it.

Texas was owned by Mexico. Since 1821, the Mexicans had granted land to Americans. Now there were about 30,000 Americans living in Texas.

Davy traveled to Texas with some friends. The Red River Valley in east Texas delighted him. Right away he made up his mind to settle there. The fields were rich and green. There was plenty of timber, and the water was sparkling clear and cold. Buffalo passed through going north or south as the seasons changed.

"Texas is the garden spot of the world," Davy wrote to his daughter. "It has the best land and prospects for health I ever saw. It's worth a fortune to any man to come here. There is a world of country to settle."

Davy planned to move his family to Texas. He felt that trouble was brewing in the big territory, but he was looking to the future. He took the oath of allegiance to the Texas government and joined the volunteer militia. This would allow him to vote and hold office.

Mexico was too busy with revolutions inside its own borders to manage the Texas lands. But in the early 1830's it tried to strengthen its rule over the settlers. First, it forbade slavery. Then it tried to stop more United States settlers from coming in. The Texans rebelled. They wanted their independence.

Santa Anna, the new president of Mexico, decided to punish them. With nearly 3,000 men, he marched toward San Antonio. Davy heard the bad news.

"That's where that little fort is, isn't it?" he said to one of his friends.

"Yes," the friend replied. "The fort is called the Alamo. It used to be an old Spanish mission. Colonel Jim Bowie has gone to help the men there. But they need more help badly."

"What are we waiting for?" said Davy.

A small party was soon on its way. The men reached the Alamo in February. Inside the fort, they found about 150 men in good spirits. They were all determined to fight for "liberty or death." Colonel William Travis was in command. He assigned each man to a special place. All hope of further help had gone.

"Colonel Bowie, have you got that rib-tickler of yours ready?" Davy asked.

"You could tickle a fellow's ribs right smart with that without making him laugh."

Bowie grinned. He knew Davy was referring to the knife that he had designed. He used it for skinning bears and Indians.

"It's ready, Colonel Crockett," Bowie said. "Now when are those Mexican varmints going to show themselves?"

The words were hardly out of his mouth when the shout rang out, "Here they come! To your stations!"

The men rushed to their places. Blasts from the cannon filled the air.

"Show your faces so Old Betsy and me can get a bead on you," shouted Davy.

Old Betsy was soon hitting her targets.

But Davy and the men in the Alamo were greatly outnumbered. Santa Anna's men swept into the fort. On they came, past the stacked mattresses and sandbags that sheltered the brave defenders. Their bayonets were drawn. Bodies were tossed aside like so much straw. The mass slaughter was watched by each man until it reached him.

Davy Crockett and Jim Bowie, with all the others, fought on bravely until the last man fell.

Davy lay dead, Old Betsy by his side. But Davy had not died in vain.

"Remember the Alamo!" became the cry that rallied and united the Texas territory. General Sam Houston and his men defeated the Mexicans and Santa Anna was taken prisoner.

"Liberty or death!" had been the last cry at the Alamo. Davy Crockett had stuck to his slogan, "Be sure you're right, then go ahead!"

Davy Crockett was surely a great frontiersman, and his spirit will live forever.